ALL ABOUT ME
by
Kayli Gizel

All About Me: Growing Up With Turner Syndrome and
Nonverbal Learning Disabilities
Written by Kayli Gizel, Illustrations by Kayli Gizel and Jim Boughton
© 2004 Maple Leaf Center

Published and distributed by:

Maple Leaf Center
270 Olde Pine Lane
Wallingford, VT   USA 05773
(802) 446-3601
www.MapleLeafCenter.com
MapleLeaf@vermontel.net

Printed in Canada

Hard Cover: ISBN 0-9759850-0-0
Soft Cover: ISBN 0-9759850-1-9
Library of Congress Control Number: 2004110337

This book is dedicated to my mother,
who taught me that it doesn't matter if I'm different.

Foreword

Kayli Gizel is an exceptional young lady. I had the pleasure of meeting Kayli and her mother at the annual national conference of the Turner Syndrome Society. While exchanging stories of this challenging disorder her mother told me about a book Kayli had written for a school-wide writing project. Kayli's book, detailed her experiences growing up with Turner Syndrome. Presented here is Kayli's story of her search for self-understanding complete with her own illustrations that have been enhanced by artist James Boughton.

Turner Syndrome is a rare genetic disorder first defined by William Turner in the 1930s. This disorder only affects females and is caused by the loss of all or parts of the second X chromosome. Symptoms include reduced height as well as other physical abnormalities. Cognitively these individuals often struggle with visual-spatial cognition, working memory, arithmetic, and social and emotional difficulties. Virtually all individuals with Turner Syndrome have the assets and deficits found in Nonverbal Learning Disabilities (NLD). Symptoms of NLD are also seen in individuals with several disorders, including, Callosal Agenesis, Asperger's Syndrome, Velocardialfacial Syndrome, Williams Syndrome, and deLange Syndrome.

The label of Nonverbal Learning Disabilities, first coined by Dr. Myklebust in 1975, and later extensively researched by Dr. Byron P. Rourke (Windsor, Ontario, Canada), has a distinct neuropsychological presentation. Dr. Rourke's research has given us insight into how to identify and overcome the various challenges that are faced by individuals with NLD.

I hope that you enjoy Kayli's story as much as I have. Kayli's book is an inspiration, not just to those who strive to cope with Turner Syndrome and/or NLD, but to anyone who has struggled with being different.

Dean J.M. Mooney, Ph.D., NCSP

Maple Leaf Clinical Services
270 Olde Pine Lane
Wallingford, Vermont, USA 05773
(802) 446-3577
www.MapleLeafClinical.com
MLCS@vermontel.net

Hi there, I'm Kayli Gizel!
I would like to tell you about myself.
So sit back and enjoy, "All About Me".

My name is Kayli Gizel.
I was born with a genetic condition called Turner Syndrome.

When we are born, we have specific chromosomes.
A boy will usually have chromosomes XY. The Y chromosome gives
a boy his 'male' characteristics.

A girl is usually born with XX chromosomes.
The second X gives a girl her 'female' characteristics.

XX

XY

In Turner Syndrome, the second X is either missing or damaged. If it is missing, the girl has Turner Syndrome XO.

If only part of the second X is missing, then the girl is Turner Syndrome Mosaic.

I have Turner Syndrome Mosaic. Some of my cells have whole XX, and some of my cells are Xiq, meaning parts of the second X are missing.

XO

Xiq

Chromosomes are made up of bands of genes. Each gene gives us a specific physical or personality characteristic. For example, I have a gene for blue eyes.

There are scientists working on a very exciting experiment called the Human Genome Project. These scientists are working to identify which genes perform what functions in our bodies. For people like me who have missing genes, this is very, very exciting!

For now, there is no way for me to know exactly all of the characteristics that I will have because of the parts of my genes that are missing. What we do know is that almost all of the girls with Turner Syndrome have a missing Shox gene. The Shox gene is the gene that makes people grow. Even though we are missing this gene, we still grow, but only a little each year.

When I was born, I was only 18 inches long. The smallest pajamas hung over my feet and my hands. I grew slowly. At six months of age, I wore clothes for a six month old. Most six month olds wear clothes for a nine or twelve month old. By the time I was three years old, I was only 33 inches tall. The average three year old is 37 inches tall. I continued to grow slowly.

I started kindergarten at a private school. All of the students wore a uniform. The smallest jumper I could get still hung down to the top of my socks. My small backpack was so huge that it hung down below my back. I was the smallest kid in the class. The kids realized that I was different and started to tease me. They called me chicken and shorty. This made me feel very angry and I wanted to hurt them, but I didn't. No one played with me during recess or play time. I was left out most of the time. This made me feel sad.

My mom sat me down and told me about Turner Syndrome. She told me that I would probably always be the shortest in my class. But, my mom also told me that it's not the outside that matters, but it's how you are on the inside that counts.

First grade was better. My teacher was great! She noticed that I was having trouble holding my pencil and that I didn't like to write. She also noticed that I was very smart, but had trouble getting along with other kids. She spoke to my mom about what she had noticed. So, my mom took me to see an occupational therapist. We found out that I had problems with my fine-motor skills. The therapist said that I needed occupational therapy. I loved going to OT! My therapist was very nice. We would play games and do fun things that helped make my fingers get stronger. I was so excited to go to OT that I had a hard time waiting in the waiting room. I am not a patient person!

Second grade was my worst year at school. My teacher had problems controlling our class. It was so loud that I couldn't even think. Because it was so loud, I would escape by going to the bathroom, it was quiet there. I found out later that some Turner girls have very sensitive ears. My grades dropped and I couldn't learn anything in there. It was so bad that my mom started to teach me at home at night. I was still the smallest in the class.

The kids were meaner than ever, and the names that they called me got worse. I had absolutely no friends at school at all. Two weeks before the school year was over, my teacher made a remark about me in front of the whole class. The whole class was laughing, but I was crying. That was my last day of school there, because my mom took me home and never took me back. It was during this time that my mom found some information on the computer about Turner girls having Nonverbal Learning Disabilities (NLD).

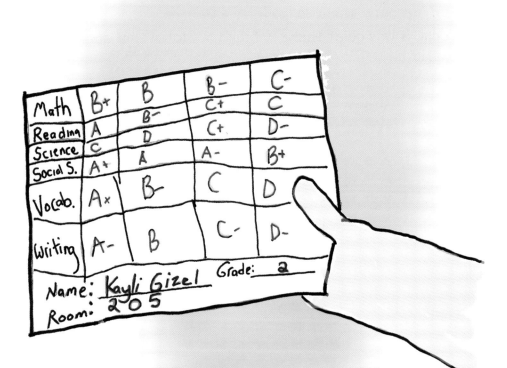

Math	B+	B	B-	C-
Reading	A	B-	C+	C
Science	C	D	C+	D-
Social S.	A+	A	A-	B+
Vocab.	Ax	B-	C	D
Writing	A-	B	C-	D-

Name: Kayli Gizel Grade: 2

Room: 205

In the fall of 2000, I started third grade (at a different school)! There was also an International Turner Syndrome Society conference held in my home state of Illinois that fall.
Mom and I attended.

For the first time, I met other Turner girls. I realized that I was not the only girl in the world with Turner Syndrome. There are many girls and women with TS. I started to not feel so different and I hardly thought about having Turner Syndrome. I attended meetings with the girls, and my mom went to lectures for the parents. We learned a lot about TS that weekend. My mom met grown women with TS who were making positive contributions to society. One of the presentations was about the connection between TS and NLD. My mom said that this lecture was like a window opening because it helped to explain so much about the things that were happening to me. This conference changed my life, and my mom's life too.

Nonverbal Learning Disabilities (NLD) occurs when the nerves that connect the two sides of the brain are missing or damaged. Individuals with NLD have trouble reading facial expressions and body language. This often causes problems with social skills, like joining in on a conversation, or joining other kids when they are playing. People would think that I was rude because I would just interrupt. I wasn't doing it on purpose. Now that I am aware of this, I try to be more careful. Even though most of the information about TS states that math can be a challenge, I seem to have a gift for math.

Well, that third grade year at school was a great year. Learning more about TS and NLD, and starting a new school had really changed my life. The kids were a lot nicer. They seemed to accept differences in other people. They still teased, but in a fun way that made me feel like part of the group.

Mom was right, I was still the smallest in my class. I was only 44 inches tall (the average third grade student is 50 inches tall), and I had almost stopped growing. I started to take human growth hormone (HGH). Ouch! There was no pill or liquid form, only a 'shot'. I had to get an injection *every* night. At first my mom gave it to me, but I didn't like it, so I learned to do it myself. I would give myself a needle in the thigh every night. I had regular visits to the endocrinologist. She is the doctor who would tell me what dose to take to help me grow. She said that without taking the HGH, I would continue to grow slowly, and might not even reach 56 inches tall as an adult. Two years on HGH helped me to grow 8 inches. I was now 52 inches tall!

I'm almost done mom.

When fourth grade started, I had friends, but I was still having trouble getting along with them. Sometimes, because of the NLD, I had trouble figuring out if people were joking or being serious. I take in all of my information verbally. If someone says something with a funny face, I just hear the words, I don't understand their face. I had a lot of trouble trying to decide what people really meant when they spoke. My mom took me to a neuropsychologist, someone who helps people with neurological (brain and nerve) learning disorders.

I have now learned to do some things that kids without NLD do naturally. I can now join in on conversations and talk on the telephone. I have learned not to interrupt, but to wait until the other person has finished speaking. I have also learned to watch movies with subtitles. Seeing all of the words at the bottom of the screen really helps me to understand what is going on much better. Sometimes, I have to ask people to re-phrase the things that they say so that I can understand their true meaning.

In fifth grade, I continued to see the neuropsychologist. Instead of meeting just with her, I met with a group of kids with problems similar to mine. We learned a lot from each other and have become good friends.

I have a lot of interests too. I have been playing the piano for a few years. I have also been dancing for six years and love to perform in the recital each year.

I have learned that being different doesn't mean something bad...it just means different, not the same. There will be times when I will have to stand up for myself because of the way others handle 'different' people. For example, my dance teacher put me in a dance with the younger girls just because of my height. I didn't think that was fair, so I told her so. They refused to change the situation, so I refused to dance in that dance. I did dance in the piece that the whole class performed together, but I did not dance with the younger girls. A person should be judged by their ability, not by their size.

If something you really wanted was on a high shelf, you might stand on a chair so you could reach it. I have learned that even though I am different, I can still do anything that anyone else can do. I can reach anything that I want to reach. I can be anything that I want to be!

Being different does help me to see the world in a way that most kids don't. I would never tease someone because they look different, have a different culture, or talk differently. I have a cousin with Cerebral Palsy. I don't treat him differently. I have a friend who is Islamic. I don't treat her differently. No matter what color, race, or religion a person is, they can still be my friend. If everyone were the same, it would be boring.

God made us all different and that's what makes each and every one of us special.

The End

...or is it the beginning?

About Turner Syndrome

Turner Syndrome (TS) is a chromosomal condition that describes girls and women with common features that are caused by complete or partial absence of the second sex chromosome.   The syndrome is named after Dr. Henry Turner, who was among the first to describe its features in the 1930s.   TS occurs in approximately 1 in 2,000 live female births.

For more information about TS, contact:

Turner Syndrome Society
www.Turner-Syndrome-US.org
14450 TC Jester, Suite 260
Houston, TX 77014
Toll Free 1-800-365-9944

About the Syndrome of Nonverbal Learning Disabilities

Nonverbal Learning Disabilities is a specific pattern of neuropsychological assets and deficits. The 'nonverbal' of NLD does not mean that these individuals are 'not' verbal. To the contrary, they are often overly verbal, not knowing when to end a conversation. They also have a tendency to interrupt to join in on a conversation. They learn best verbally, so they hear the words but may not interpret the facial or body expressions of the person who is speaking. Therefore, understanding the true meaning of what someone is saying can be a real challenge for those with NLD. As a result, they tend to suffer socially. They can get frustrated, overwhelmed, and become withdrawn. Generally they excel in spelling and reading, but struggle with reading *comprehension*, math, writing, and the sciences. By teaching the individual about their strengths and weaknesses and by putting appropriate interventions in place as early as possible, individuals with NLD can succeed!

For more information about NLD, contact:

Maple Leaf Center
270 Olde Pine Lane
Wallingford, VT 05773 USA
(802) 446-3601
www.MapleLeafCenter.com
MapleLeaf@vermontel.net

About the Human Genome Project

Technology and resources promoted by the Human Genome Project are starting to have profound impacts on biomedical research and promise to revolutionize the wider spectrum of biological research and clinical medicine. Increasingly detailed genome maps have aided researchers seeking genes associated with dozens of genetic conditions, including myotonic dystrophy, fragile X syndrome, neurofibromatosis types 1 and 2, inherited colon cancer, Alzheimer's disease, and familial breast cancer.

On the horizon is a new era of molecular medicine characterized less by treating symptoms and more by looking to the most fundamental causes of disease. Rapid and more specific diagnostic tests will make possible earlier treatment of countless maladies. Medical researchers also will be able to devise novel therapeutic regimens based on new classes of drugs, immunotherapy techniques, avoidance of environmental conditions that may trigger disease, and possible augmentation or even replacement of defective genes through gene therapy.

For more information about this Project, log onto the following website that has information geared especially for students:

www.ornl.gov/sci/techresources/Human_Genome/project/
benefits.shtml

Kayli Gizel was born on July 11, 1992. Shortly after her birth, she was diagnosed with Turner Syndrome Mosaic. She has been aware of her diagnosis since she was about five years old, when she began to really notice her height difference. She currently takes an active role in her health management. She also is a strong advocate for herself at school with regard to her NLD issues. She consistently makes A's and B's in school.

Kayli has been a dancer since she was five years old and has taken ballet, jazz, tap, and hip-hop. Her favorite of these is tap. She participates in a yearly dance recital. Kayli also has a strong interest in acting, has taken acting classes, and has performed on stage in two plays. She loves to watch movies. She can tell you the names of the actors and can usually list all of their other movies too!

Kayli hopes that this book will help other girls who may be struggling with their diagnosis of Turner Syndrome and/or NLD. Even though we are all different, we are all human beings and need to treat each other with respect and dignity.

Where Is She Now?

At the time of publishing (summer 2004), Kayli is twelve years old, and preparing to enter the seventh grade. She will be continuing with both dance and acting classes. She continues with daily human growth hormone (HGH) therapy and is 55 inches tall. By monitoring Kayli's bone age, and anticipating the time that hormonal replacement therapy will begin, the endocrinologist is predicting her final height to be 60 inches (5 feet) tall.

Kayli has a Section 504 educational plan in place, in her school file, to accommodate the issues related to her Nonverbal Learning Disabilities (NLD). In spite of being a person with NLD, she scored past the eighth grade level in vocabulary and math computation, and at the eighth grade level on reading comprehension on her sixth grade standardized achievement testing. Kayli is proof positive that people with Turner Syndrome and/or NLD can succeed.

Glossary of Terms

Cerebral Palsy:
Weakness and lack of coordination of the muscles, resulting from damage to the brain, usually at or before birth.

Chromosome:
A small body in all living cells, usually contained in a nucleus and composed mainly of DNA. It carries the genes that determine heredity.

Different:
Unlike in form, quality, amount, or nature.

Fine-motor:
Small, detailed movements, such as holding a pencil, cutting with scissors, drawing with crayons.

Gene:
A segment of DNA, located at a particular point on a chromosome, that determines hereditary characteristics. Hair and eye color in human beings are characteristics controlled by genes.

Genome:
The complete genetic information of an organism. In a cell with a nucleus, the genome includes one member from each pair of chromosomes. In a cell without a nucleus, the genome is the single chromosome.

Interrupt:
To hinder or stop the action of; break in on.

Literal:
Following the usual or exact meaning of a word or group of words.

Mosaic:
1. a picture or design made on a surface by fitting and cementing together small colored pieces; 2. an organism or a part having adjacent cells or tissues of different genetic types.

Re-phrase:
Repeat in a different way to enhance understanding.